M000309929

Welcome to the Lord's Table

Richard A. Melheim

CONCORDIA PUBLISHING HOUSE • SAINT LOUIS

Concordia
Publishing House
www.cph.org

Copyright © 1993 Concordia Publishing House
3558 South Jefferson Avenue, St. Louis, MO 63118-3968

All rights reserved. No part of this publication may be reproduced, stored in a retrieval system, transmitted, in any form or by any means, electronic, mechanical, photocopying, recording, or otherwise, without the prior written permission of Concordia Publishing House.

Scripture taken from the Revised Standard Version of the Bible, copyrighted 1946, 1952, © 1971, 19 Used by permission.

Manufactured in the United States of America

5 6 7 8 9 10 11 12   13 12 11 10 09 08 07 06

Contents

How can it be that wafer thin
is now the body of my Lord?
How can it be that bitter wine
conveys to me his saving blood?

How can it be that I, though lost,
would dare to gaze, my eyes not hide?
How can it be that I, though stained,
could dare to inch toward Jesus' side?

How can it be he comes to me
in, with, and under bread and wine?
The mystery that I should taste
the great and serious joy that's mine?

How can it be the living Christ?
the healing touch? the life restored?
How can it be? I do not know.
But in real presence,
Jesus Lord,
come.

How Can It Be?

Bread, wine, body, blood, forgiveness. What does it all mean? And how does it fit together? The invisible, almighty Son of God says that his body and blood are in simple fruits of the earth. The great and unknowable Creator of the universe directs our attention to a cup, to a loaf. What is this riddle, this mystery?

Television and radio waves bombard us wherever we go. We can't see them, hear them, or feel them. They certainly don't interfere with our everyday lives. Most of us don't know how they work. They're a bit of a mystery. Much of the time we don't even give them a second thought. They fly past us unnoticed until and unless we have a mechanism to receive those waves and turn them into something understandable like sight and sound.

Like the unseen radio waves, our God is invisible to us. God surrounds and permeates all of life, yet we can't see, hear, or physically feel him. We can even go through our days without giving the Almighty God a second thought. We needed God himself to break into our lives, to touch our lives and make himself known to us. As finite beings who are by nature not tuned to God, we needed a great and powerful mechanism to tune in to the infinite.

Jesus Christ became flesh and blood exactly for that purpose. Everything he did, everything he taught, all that he was reflected the will and the wonder of our marvelous Creator. By coming as our Savior, Jesus showed us (who have never seen God) "the light of the knowledge of the glory of God" (2 Corinthians 4:6) by turning his face toward us in love and forgiveness and invitation. Jesus has not only made the unknowable known and the invisible visible, he has touched us with the gracious presence of God.

And on the night in which he was betrayed, to give us a sign of his grace that we could touch, our Lord sat down to supper with his friends, shared with them a piece of bread and a sip of wine, and called them "my body," "my blood." Today, we receive the same food, we hear the same words: Christ gives us himself for our forgiveness. With the first disciples, we share in a mystery. Through faith in God's promise we receive the gifts of forgiveness, life, and salvation. For in, with, and under the bread and wine we who are finite have now been given an infinite gift: the ability to see, to touch, and to know the real presence of the Jesus Christ—in the bread, with the wine.

Table Talk

In our fast-paced, rat-race, microwaveable minute-rice world, families don't always have the chance to share meals together. If mom or dad is late from work, Billie has a date, Jeri's on a water and cardboard diet, Chris has to catch a ride to his karate lesson, and little Frieda is overdue at her Junior Chipmunk meeting, not much communicating takes place around the dinner table. Who has time for such quaint notions as family meals anymore? Who takes time?

Only those who make it a priority.

When is there time for the larger Christian community to gather, celebrate, and reestablish who they are and to whom they belong? When is there time to share the meaning of life together as God's people and bathe in the Creator's presence?

The Lutheran family comes to the table regularly to share a meal. They make it a priority. It is a meal that Jesus Christ himself calls us to share. He invites us to this table in order that we might stay in touch with God, with our brothers and sisters, and with ourselves. In the supper Christ serves as both giver and gift, master and servant, host and feast. Through it he brings forgiveness of sins, life, and salvation. This meal has many different names and is celebrated in many different ways. The Lutheran church most often calls it Holy Communion.

Holy What?

Imagine knowing nothing about the practice of Holy Communion and for the first time hearing terms like *eating Christ's body* and *drinking his blood.* Without a basic understanding of what Communion is, this sacrament sounds weird, spooky, and mysterious. Even with an understanding of what Jesus has said and done for us, this beautiful, personal gift of the Lord is still a mystery. As an old hymn puts it:

> . . . this mystery I ponder, Filling all my soul with wonder
> . . . . These great mysteries unsounded Are by God alone expounded.
>
> *The Lutheran Hymnal* 305:5–6

Holy Communion is celebrated with many different practices and traditions and has been given many explanations. Some see it as a mere representation of Christ's body and blood. Others talk about the bread and wine actually being changed into the physical flesh of Christ each time the elements are consecrated. Some speak of a symbolic unity being the point of the meal. Others see Holy Communion as a sacrifice, offered to God for our forgiveness. Still others look at it as basically an exercise in remembering a fallen leader who is lost and gone forever.

But what is Holy Communion? Where did it come from? How should we understand it? And why should we participate in it? An informed Christian will want to ask these questions and study the Scriptures carefully before making any decisions about it. This little book will help you do just that.

CHAPTER 1

The Origin of Holy Communion

The Night He Was Betrayed

Jesus understood the trouble we were in. Just as darkness cannot enter the presence of light, so sinful humanity could not begin to approach the presence of the perfect God. The world was lost unless a way could be found to blot out human sin and restore people to God. A holy and perfect payment had to be made; a spotless sacrifice had to be offered to take away the sin of the world. And so, in the power of love, God did the one thing that could rescue us from our dilemma. Coming to us in the person of Jesus Christ, God gave us the one gift with the power to release us from the penalty of sin. Jesus gave us himself, his whole self, and took our sins with him to the cross.

Sound fantastic? It is.

And before he died, in order to help his followers experience the forgiveness and touch of his presence until his return, Jesus gave the gift of Communion. This is how it happened:

The Passover

It all started during the time of the Passover Festival. Jesus, being a devout Jew who celebrated the festivals of God's saving acts with reverence, asked two of his disciples to prepare the place where he and all the disciples would share the Passover meal. They went into town as he had directed them, found an upstairs room, and prepared the traditional feast of unleavened (flat) bread, bitter herbs dipped in salt water, roast lamb, and red wine mixed with water.

The Passover Festival was one of the central celebrations of God's people. It marked the pivotal saving act of God in history when the Hebrew nation was freed from slavery in Egypt. All over Jerusalem that night, people were gathering with families and friends to share the meal, pray, sing the ancient songs, and retell the story of how the angel of death "passed over" their houses but killed the firstborn sons of Egypt. (After the angel of death did his business, Pharaoh was more than willing to let his slaves go.) The Passover was a holy celebration set aside to recount the stories of slavery, to remember the saving acts of God, and to praise the Almighty for the miracle of freedom.

As he prepared to join in the Passover celebration that evening, Jesus understood that he was about to die. He knew that his friends would all soon desert him and run off, frightened and alone. He wanted to give these followers a connection to himself that could be theirs throughout life—a gift that would allow them to keep hope and remain strong, even in the face of the dark days ahead. So he took this ancient festival supper of remembrance and changed it into a new meal of remembrance and hope. Reclining at the low table (as was the custom in that part of the world), our Lord thanked God, ate, and then said the words that were to make the Passover bread and wine into a celebration that would be sacred to the Christian church on into the centuries.

The Bread

After supper Jesus took a piece of bread, blessed it, broke it, and gave it to his disciples, telling them, "This is my body, which is given for you."

In those days bread held a central role in both diet and tradition. It was called the staff of life because it was the main food that supported life. Without bread the people would die. Because of its important role, bread was treated with respect. People wouldn't think of cutting a loaf with a knife. They considered cutting bread to be barbaric. It would be like insulting the very thing that gave them life—like showing disdain for the gift that sustained them. Instead of cutting it, they would break it after reverently giving thanks to God for providing it.

"Blessed are you, Lord God, King of the universe, who brings forth bread from the earth" was the common table prayer of the Jewish people. They knew bread was God's gift for their lives. When the Israelites hungered in the wilderness, God fed them bread from heaven or "manna." (In Hebrew the word means "What is it?" The Israelites had looked out of their tents in the morning and asked literally, "What's that?") Ancient peoples knew what it was like to be without bread—to be hungry. Their lives were very different from ours today. If hungry, they couldn't simply run down to the local burger palace and grab a cheese burger or a chili dog to go. If hungry, they would have to work long, hard hours in the fields for what they ate. Thus, their great respect for bread. For them to pray "give us this day our daily bread" meant a lot. It wasn't simply asking God to give them a piece of toast. It was asking God to sustain their very lives.

So, on that last night with his friends, when Jesus took the bread saying, "This is my body," he was dealing with the center and source of life. And when we call Jesus "the living bread from heaven" who feeds his guests well, we are not speaking about an incidental part of life, but its center and source.

The disciples shared that loaf like a family sharing a meal. And in the final breaking of bread with their Lord, they were given both strength for what would lie ahead and a foretaste of the presence they would know on into eternity.

"Take, eat," Jesus said. "This is my body, which is given for you. This do in remembrance of me."

From that Passover night on, whenever the followers of Jesus ate together they were not simply to remember the rescue from slavery in Egypt. They would now understand and recall the greatest saving act of all time: the day when God set up a means to save the whole world from sin through this Jesus who called himself their friend—who called himself the "bread of life" (John 6:35).

The Wine

Wine had an important place in the Jewish culture as well. It was used for both the common and the uncommon, for everyday meals as well as celebrations and sacrifices. Whenever it was used, a prayer was offered thanking God: "Blessed are you, Lord God, King of the universe, for you have given us the fruit of the vine."

Jesus called the wine his blood. This was strange language, even for Jesus to use. To people in that culture blood was a mysterious and powerful symbol, always held with great respect. The blood of an animal was treated as the very life of that animal. Blood was considered to hold the power that kept a body functioning. (This made sense: If you drained all the blood out of an animal, its body didn't function too well!) The life force of a being was thought to be held in the blood. To some, the life force *was* the blood. Eating or sacrificing a beast without first returning its blood to the soil was considered an insult to the Creator and was forbidden by the ceremonial law. The blood (the life) had to be returned to God before an animal's flesh could be used. Blood was life, and all life belonged to God.

After supper, following the breaking of the bread, Jesus offered the blessing for the wine but then added some deep and uncommon words. The statement was as mystical as it was revolutionary. He told his friends: "Drink of it, all of you; this is my blood of the covenant, which is poured out for many for the forgiveness of sins"

(Matthew 26:27–28). Or as Luke records it, "This cup . . . is the new covenant in my blood" (22:20). In calling that cup the new covenant (way to have a relationship with God) in his blood, Jesus was announcing a radical change in the way people were now to relate to God.

In talking about a new covenant, Jesus was using language that Jeremiah had used six centuries earlier:

> "Behold, the days are coming, says the Lord, when I will make a *new covenant* with the house of Israel and the house of Judah, not like the covenant which I made with their fathers . . . my covenant which they broke, though I was their husband, says the Lord. But this is the covenant which I will make with the house of Israel after those days, says the Lord: I will put my law within them, and I will write it upon their hearts; and I will be their God, and they shall be my people. . . . I will forgive their iniquity, and I will remember their sin no more."
>
> Jeremiah 31:31–34

In former days, the days of the old covenant, God told his people that blood had to be shed for their sins to be forgiven. That usually meant they were to bring a valuable animal up to the altar where it was sacrificed. Blood had to be shed—a life had to be taken—to pay the penalty for sins. The sacrificial system was the way that God had provided for his old covenant people to show sorrow and to receive forgiveness.

By calling the wine his blood and stating that it was to be shed for the forgiveness of sins, Jesus was announcing a new covenant. He was blowing the old sacrificial system apart—by fulfilling it! Under this new covenant, Jesus' own blood would be the final and complete sacrifice for all time. Instead of a spotless lamb, Christ was the sacrifice. In Jesus' death for us as the final sacrifice of all, we see God's will for us. We see God forgiving our iniquity and remembering our sins no more. That's quite a claim! But remember John the Baptist's words after Jesus' Baptism: "Behold, the Lamb of God, who takes away the sin of the world!" (John 1:29).

The Rest of the Story

"This is my body. . . . my blood. . . ." The disciples (who had never understood what Jesus meant about being betrayed, suffering, dying, and rising) could not have fully realized all that Jesus meant when he talked about his body "given for you," his blood "shed for you." But with those simple, radical words Jesus announced a change in the old order.

The Lord ended with this charge: "This do in remembrance of me." The disciples finished dinner, sang some songs, and then went out into the night. In the few short hours that were to follow, Jesus would be betrayed by Judas, deserted by his closest friends, arrested, mocked in a secret trial, sentenced to death, hung on a cross, and laid in a borrowed grave.

But that wasn't the end.

The meal would have disappeared from the pages of history if that had been the end of the story. This announcement of a new order would have been a joke if Christ had remained in the grave. Our lives, our future, our world would be hopelessly lost if the crucifixion had ended it all. But it didn't.

You know the rest of the story. The stone was rolled away from the tomb. The body was gone. Jesus was alive! He had risen! Christ had offered his own life, his whole self in love for a lost world. It was God's plan all along. And now God had raised him up.

Today, as we gather to remember Jesus' sacrifice, we take his words "This do in remembrance of me" seriously. We receive the meal and accept it as a "heavenly table" by which we feed on forgiveness and life. We receive the body and blood of the Lord of life himself when we take the bread and wine. And remembering his promise to one day return to share the eternal victory feast with all who trust in him, we are filled with a great and serious joy!

From Last Supper to Lord's Supper

Early Christians shared in the Lord's Supper often. At first it was celebrated as a regular meal. Believers simply met, ate together, and waited for their Lord's return. These followers of Jesus were living a continual Passover, experiencing not just the memory of Jesus, but the reality of the risen Christ. Certainly, the disciples knew that each time they gathered, their risen Lord and friend, Jesus, was really present; in Matthew 18:20 he had promised that wherever two or three would gather in his name, he'd be there with them. But in a special and wonderful way he was present in this meal. This gave their lives a joy even as they faced hardships. It was this love and joy that drew others to them like a magnet.

"Day by day, attending the temple together and breaking bread in their homes, they partook of food with glad and generous hearts, praising God and having favor with all the people. And the Lord added to their number day by day those who were being saved" (Acts 2:46–47).

End of the Potluck

For a while the supper was part of a "full meal deal." Christians in a community would bring food and gather to share it—much like a church potluck. They would eat their food all together and then take a special time to share the bread and wine in Christ's honor. This went on in a loving, communal atmosphere for a while. But it didn't last long. It seems that some of the richer folks wouldn't share their food with their poorer brothers and sisters. Some wouldn't wait for others to come but would hog down all the food (and wine!) themselves before anyone else arrived. In his writings to the church

17

at Corinth, Paul revealed the struggle he had with the Christians who were eating selfishly. We don't know all the details of the history, but within the first century of the early Christian church, the Lord's Supper was turned into a separate memorial service apart from the potluck dinners of the congregation.

The Meal Today

Today Christians all over the world take Jesus' command "this do in remembrance of me" seriously. Every Sunday in every corner of the world millions of followers of the Carpenter of Galilee gather to receive his gifts by remembering his words and sharing in the bread and the wine. We come looking for Jesus Christ to "nourish our weak souls that they may flourish" (*Lutheran Worship* 238:1). We come asking Christ to be with us, just as he was with the disciples on that Passover night. We come asking Christ to strengthen us and to give us the gift of forgiveness. We kneel to take the bread and wine that Jesus still calls his body and his blood. We remember his words "for you for the forgiveness of sins" and pray for cleansing, strength, and assurance. And we rise, filled with the presence of the living God and the power to start again.

Thought Time

1. Read about the Passover in Exodus 12:21–32. How does this central saving act in the Old Testament relate to Holy Communion?

2. How does the sacrifice of animals (in the days of the old covenant) relate to the sacrifice of Christ?

3. Bread and wine had important roles in Jesus' culture. How do the roles of these two elements in the ancient world enrich our modern understanding of Holy Communion?

4. Write a short essay finishing this sentence: Forgiveness of sins is essential because without it . . .

18

CHAPTER 2

The Sacraments
A Lutheran Perspective

A sacrament, as the Lutheran church defines it, is a special gift of God's forgiving grace to us. We usually confine the word *sacrament*—which originally meant "sacred word" or "sacred oath"—to the sacred acts of God to us which were instituted by Christ and performed with a physical element. In all of Christ's gifts to us, we see two such sacred acts—Baptism and Holy Communion—fitting this definition.

Beginning and Belonging

Baptism is the sacrament of beginning and belonging. Jesus commanded it in Matthew 28:19 when he said: "Go therefore and make disciples of all nations, baptizing them in the name of the Father and of the Son and of the Holy Spirit."

The gift of grace in Baptism comes as the new Christian becomes one with the body of Christ and is joined to Jesus' death and resurrection. The gift of grace in Baptism is forgiveness of sin and adoption into God's family. Water, the physical element, serves as a washing of cleansing and rebirth. Lutherans see baptismal water as more than a mere symbol. Together with God's Word and promise, this water ushers in the beginning of our eternal life with God.

Forgiving and Restoring

Communion is the sacrament of forgiving and restoring. It was instituted by Jesus, as three of the four gospels and Paul's first letter to the Corinthians record, when he said: "Take, eat. . . . This do in remembrance of me." According to Martin Luther, the gifts of grace in Communion are forgiveness of sins, life, and salvation (Small Catechism).

Lutherans see the bread and wine as more than mere representations of Christ. In these elements, with these elements, under these elements, hidden in mystery beyond our comprehension, Christ's body and blood are really given to his people. Through this sacrament Jesus brings his Spirit of love, power, forgiveness, and assurance into our lives; indeed, he places his love, power, forgiveness, and assurance on our lips. In more than a sentimental sense, Christ touches our very being.

When a baby enters the world, it must be fed and nurtured in order to survive. Without food, warmth, protection, and plenty of love, a child will not last long. Just as the Sacrament of Baptism is like a new birth, the Sacrament of Holy Communion is the food and care that help nurture and sustain the Christian life. In this sacrament, Christ assures us of our forgiveness and bonds us to a family of caring people so that we can mature and grow strong in knowledge, love, and service.

The Real Presence of Christ

How can Christ's body and blood be truly present in the bread and wine? Do these elements change into flesh and blood? Some churches teach that they do. (They call it transubstantiation.) Was Jesus speaking only symbolically about the bread and wine? Some churches teach that he was. Lutherans look to Christ's words "This is my body. . . . my blood" and see a mystery. Jesus didn't say, "This is like my body and blood." He said, "This is . . ."

Where is Jesus? Jesus, as God, is certainly present everywhere. More than that, he promises to be present with his grace wherever his people gather. Jesus told his disciples in Matthew 18:20: "Where two or three are gathered in my name, there am I in the midst of them." There is no reason, therefore, to draw back from Jesus' very special promise of the presence of his body and blood with grace and forgiveness in the bread and wine.

Lutherans believe that Jesus is indeed present as he said, in a unique and meaningful way in the bread and the wine. They describe this mystery with the term *real presence*. When we come with a confessing heart, seeking his presence, and take the bread and wine, we don't see the bread and wine change into the physical flesh and blood of Christ. But we believe, as Jesus told us, that we are receiving more than a simple memory of Christ far away. Tasting and touching these simple elements, we believe that the living Jesus Christ, the Son of God, is really present in the bread and wine and touches us in a special and tangible way.

Luther's Small Teaching

Martin Luther felt that instruction in the faith should be a family matter. There were no Sunday schools in his day to teach young people. Most of them, to learn anything at all about Christianity, would have to learn at home from their families.

In 1529, in order to assist parents in the instruction of their children (and to subtly teach the parents a few things at the same time), Luther prepared a short and simple instruction booklet. This small teaching, or catechism, included sections on everything he considered basic to an understanding of the Christian faith. The Sacraments of Baptism and Communion are explained, along with brief descriptions of the meanings of the Ten Commandments, the Apostles' Creed, the Lord's Prayer, and Confession and Absolution (called the Office of the Keys). Take a moment and page through a copy of Luther's Small Catechism to familiarize yourself with its content and approach.

The Words of Institution

In an effort to clarify the events of the Last Supper, Luther used a compilation that combined the four accounts of that special night (Matthew 26:26–29; Mark 14:22–25; Luke 22:14–20; and 1 Corinthians 11:23–26) into one statement. These words that Christ used to start (institute) the Sacrament are now called the "Words of Institution" by the church.

Read the Words of Institution from the Small Catechism. Then look up the Bible passages above. How is each unique? How are they similar?

The Elements Alone

If we were to remove the words of Christ "This is my body. . . . my blood . . . given and shed for you for the forgiveness of sins," the bread and wine would be nothing more than bread and wine. We could eat them and they would have no more effect on us than a taco or a can of soda pop. It is God's Word given *with* the elements that makes them alive. It is God's Word given *with* the bread and wine that brings the risen Christ into our midst, gives forgiveness, and strengthens our faith and our love for one another.

Jesus is the embodiment of God's Word among us— God in flesh. In John 1:1 Jesus is called the Word of God—God's message of salvation to us. Through this sacrament the living Word comes to us embodied in bread and wine, proclaimed in the words "given and shed for you for the forgiveness of sins." God in our midst—that was the whole purpose of Christ's coming in the first place. He came to be one of us, to be one with us, to be one for us. As we share in his meal, Jesus' message and meaning come to us again. In his presence, sustained by his forgiveness, we find the peace to make us one with ourselves, one with the world, and one with our God.

Thought Time

1. Read through the five basic questions Luther asked and answered about Holy Communion in his Small Catechism. What stands out to you? Do you see anything you hadn't noticed before?

2. Take the Holy Communion section of the Small Catechism and create an exercise to help you commit it to memory. You may wish to do the following:
- Rewrite it in your own words
- Copy down every other word, then fill in the blanks
- Write a short paragraph discussing why each question is important
- Use the section as a meditative personal devotion each day for a week

CHAPTER 3

The Richness of the Gift

Martin Luther came up with a concise definition of Communion in his Small Catechism. He described it as "the true body and blood of our Lord Jesus Christ under the bread and wine, instituted by Christ himself for us Christians to eat and to drink." Simple, eh?

It may be simple in essence. But there is a richness and a variety in the biblical descriptions of Holy Communion that keep us from limiting its meaning and power to however simple a definition. Look through your hymnal and you will find a variety of descriptions and names for the Supper. There are many different traditions and ceremonies for celebrating Holy Communion within the Christian community. There are many terms for the meal and ways to describe the Sacrament's impact on us. No one method, term, or description captures all that Scripture teaches about this wonderful meal. None expresses the richness of our Lord's Supper in totality, but all combine to give a breadth and depth to our Lutheran understanding of the Sacrament.

Variations in Terms

There are many names used for this special meal. People of different backgrounds and traditions may call it one of these:

- Communion or Holy Communion
- Eucharist (YOU-car-ist)
- Lord's Supper
- Breaking of the Bread
- Sacrament of the Altar

The term *Communion* conveys the idea of the special unity we experience in the meal. St. Paul described this unity in 1 Corinthians 10:16 using a word that can be translated "fellowship" or "communion." The words *Communion* and *Holy Communion* stress the sacred closeness we share with God and with our brothers and sisters in Christ. The word *Communion* can be broken into two parts. In Latin the *com* means "with." *Union* is simple enough to understand. It stresses the oneness Christians share in Christ's love.

Eucharist is a Greek term that was used by Christian writers from the second century on. It was the favorite term of the early church because it stressed the thanks and joy that accompany this gift of life. *Eucharist* literally means "good thanksgiving."

The term *Lord's Supper* is used in the Bible only by Paul. The apostle wanted to point to Jesus as being the host of the meal. It is truly his supper, where he gives his whole life to us. In this special meal he serves us the feast of forgiveness, life, and salvation.

Breaking of the Bread is used in Luke and Acts. It first referred both to the sacramental meal and to the common potlucks of the early church. Through time it has come to be used specifically for the Sacrament and the fact that we break bread together as the family of God. When we break bread with someone, we show our acceptance of that person. Breaking bread together, we are receiving each other as family.

Sometimes the meal is called the *Sacrament of the Altar.* In Old Testament times sacrifices were made to God on the altar. Now we go to the altar to receive and remember God's once-and-for-all sacrifice for us.

Variations in Descriptions

Aside from a variety of terms for the meal, there are also a number of ways to describe its meaning. Lutherans see these not as exclusive, but as adding a richness to the meal. Some descriptions include these:

- A memorial
- A fellowship meal
- A thanksgiving
- A feast of anticipation
- A mystery

Again, the Lord's Supper is all of these in some way, shape, or form. But no term explains the Sacrament in its totality.

The meal is a *memorial* in that we do it in remembrance of Jesus. We share in it to honor his memory. This is what he asked of us. We celebrate and recall the events of his life, death, and resurrection as we take the bread and wine. Thus, it serves as a memorial. But it is much more than a mere memorial. For as we recount Christ's saving act and take it to heart, his sacrifice for us touches us. His story becomes our story, and we pray that it will have an effect on everything we do, everything we are. This meal, then, is not simply a mental recollection or a spiritual exercise. You "adorn yourself with gladness" because "he, though heavenly, high, and holy, deigns to dwell with you most lowly" (*Lutheran Worship* 239:1).

Communion is a *fellowship meal* in that it allows us to share a special closeness with both our risen Lord and his family, the church. In Christ we find the power to love and care for all people as brothers and sisters. Kneeling together at the table, our divisions and prejudices should dissolve. We cannot truly open our heart before God and yet rise from the altar still enemies with the person who has knelt beside us. When we come together before God, we come to know all people as precious ones for whom Jesus died. Or as Martin Luther said it in his Communion hymn:

> May God bestow on us his grace and favor
> To please him with our behavior
> And live together here in love and union
> Nor repent this blest communion.
>   O Lord, have mercy!
> Let not your good Spirit forsake us,

But that heavenly-minded he make us;
Give your Church, Lord, to see
Days of peace and unity.
   O Lord, have mercy!

The Supper can also be understood as a *thanksgiving*. It is an occasion for the whole church to reflect on the greatness of God's love and to thank and praise our Creator and Savior for the abundance of his gifts to us. Just as the disciples broke bread together with thankful hearts, we, too, give thanks for the marvelous gifts of grace God sets before us.

Holy Communion is also a *feast of anticipation*. In it we look forward to the greatest party the world will ever know, when Christ returns to reign forever. St. Paul wrote: "For as often as you eat this bread and drink the cup, you proclaim the Lord's death until he comes" (1 Corinthians 11:26). In this holy act we celebrate the victory already won for us by the empty cross and the open tomb. We wait in joyful anticipation for that day when we will share the eternal feast with all who have gone to meet the Lord. Thus, the Supper is a feast of anticipation. But it is even more than that.

In spite of all these definitions and understandings, the Lord's Supper is still at the heart and to the heart a *mystery*. How can it be that Christ would come to us? How can it be that we could know the presence of God? How can it be that Christ could enter into the very fabric of our beings? The meal is a mystery of the hidden God coming one step from the shadows; the unknowable glimpsed; the unseeable sensed. The untouchable God touches our lips and we finite, dim-sighted mortals are allowed to taste a morsel of the feast of eternity: the true grace, the pure peace, the perfect presence of God. How can it be? It is a mystery.

Variations in Bread

As mentioned in chapter 1, until Holy Communion moved from the "potluck" stage to the Sunday service we have today, the meal looked like a church picnic. People would gather to share the unity and community of a common meal that included a regular supper and a time for sharing the bread and wine. As years passed, Holy Communion was reserved more and more for the worship service. The elements that were used changed in shape and form over time as well. Instead of people bringing loaves from home and wine from their cellars to the service, churches began to provide these elements.

About eight or nine hundred years ago, mostly for convenience sake, loaves of bread were replaced with thin, bite-sized wafers. These were easier to handle and didn't create crumbs on the church floor. Wafers continue to be used in many churches to this day. Some congregations use flat bread. Others have gone back to the early-church custom of serving loaves baked by their own members.

Variations in Wine

Aside from different preferences in breads, the types of wine people have used over the years have changed as well. The Passover wine that Jesus used was probably a red wine mixed with water. For centuries the church used red wine to follow Christ's example.

From time to time, some people with nothing better to do have debated which kind of wine was the right kind. Some have argued that red was the only possible way to go since that was what Jesus used. Others, who were more practical, insisted that white wine was preferred since it didn't stain the altar linens. On the other hand, some have debated whether full-strength wine, wine with water, or (virtually) nonalcoholic wine was best. The "answer" is that the Lord has not shown us that he has any interest in these questions. No one should condemn another on a question the Lord has left open. The Lord used wine. Pick your wine and live in peace. What is important is the gift he is giving and the confident assurance we have that in receiving the cup of wine he has blessed, we are receiving his blood, shed for our forgiveness.

Other Variations

Other differences have arisen as to how Holy Communion should be received. Some churches let only ordained ministers handle and distribute the elements. Others allow laypeople from the congregation to help in the physical distribution. Some traditions use small individual cups of wine that are filled before the service starts. Others fill small cups from a large cup during the distribution. Still others use a single large chalice from which all drink. They feel that this provides a stronger witness of the unity of the Christian family and retains the method Jesus himself used. Some churches have members stand at the altar railing to receive the elements. Others have them kneel. Still others pass the dish down the pew and allow people to take for themselves or give to each other.

What's Important, Anyway?

People can get so caught up in debates over forms (types of glasses, types of bread, styles of giving out the elements, etc.) that they forget the meaning of what they are doing. People will tend to prefer whatever practice they are used to or whatever they find most meaningful. The type of bread, the kind of wine, the cup that brings it to you—all of these are secondary to the point of what you are doing, why you are doing it, and just who is *really* giving the gift.

You are coming before the living Christ for forgiveness. You are coming because you desire to be restored. The gift being offered to you is from God. It is Jesus Christ really present in the bread and the wine—physically coming to you and for you. It is Christ bringing forgiveness as a gift through his very body and blood. That's what really matters more than anything else. That's what really counts.

Thought Time

1. Look over the terms used to describe Holy Communion in this chapter. Which are most familiar to you? Which are most meaningful? Why?

2. Christ was sacrificed to pay for our sins. According to Romans 12:1, what sacrifice should we offer God in return? How might we do this?

3. Finish this statement: A Christian can receive the Lord's Supper with real joy because . . .

4. Write a single, concise statement describing your understanding of Holy Communion at this moment.

CHAPTER 4

Forgiveness of Sins, Life and Salvation

Forgiveness

Sin is a serious matter. It separates us from God. It separates us from others. In a strange way, it even separates us from ourselves, for it keeps us from becoming the joyful, clear-conscienced people we were meant to be.

Even secular psychiatrists tell us that unresolved guilt can entomb a living soul and hold it tighter than the bonds of any rope or chain. Only forgiveness can remove the stain of sin from our lives. Only forgiveness can restore our broken relationships with God and others. Only forgiveness can free us from the guilt that bogs us down and the punishment we are bound to face.

Luther wrote, "Where there is forgiveness of sins, there is also life and salvation" (Small Catechism). He wasn't simply talking about some vague theoretical concept. True forgiveness is essential to our total well-being as humans. True forgiveness offers a clean start and a washing away of that guilt that can destroy us. In a very real sense, the full and complete forgiveness we receive from God in Holy Communion can heal us emotionally and spiritually. Christ came to restore fullness to the whole person. By his presence through his Sacrament we can be released from sin, guilt, shame, and all the haunting hurt that accompanies it.

Luther tells us that forgiveness of sin brings life and salvation. What did he mean? How can eating the bread and drinking the wine bring life?

In the Genesis account of Adam and Eve, everything is fine in the garden until the two of them disobey God's command. God comes and finds them running to the shadows like bugs from a suddenly overturned rock. They deny, then blame, and finally hear the word that expels them from the garden. Life in paradise was over, for the relationship with God was broken.

Can there be life—true and free life—where there is guilt and shame? Can there be life when we're feeling slimy and stained, nervous and defensive before God? when we find ourselves slinking about, running from the light, the truth?

No. We can exist with these feelings. But we cannot live the life the Lord intends for us.

In order for there to be real life, we need to be able to walk with head held high. And for that to happen, we need a clean slate with God, with others, and with our conscience.

Here's where repentance and the Lord's Supper enter beautifully.

Confession and Forgiveness

We all know the feeling when we have wronged someone and haven't mustered up the courage to say, "I'm sorry." Until we are bold enough to go hat in hand and apologize, the relationship, the feelings, and the peace remain broken. Unresolved guilt and bitterness fester and infect our whole life. Unresolved wrongs are like nasty slivers or raw sores. We can't just put a Band-Aid on them and hope they'll go away. All the time in the world won't heal such infections. Pretending they don't exist and ignoring them will only bring poison and pain. We have to clean them out, apply the proper medicine, and allow time for healing.

Admitting we were wrong is the painful but necessary first step in the healing process. Confessing our wrongness is like lancing a wound. Until we open the wound, the healing salve of forgiveness cannot work its way through. And until that forgiveness salve enters, the wound will never heal properly. Confession starts the process. Forgiveness is the salve. And health and life are the results.

Life
Life with God

Now think about your relationship to God. Have you ever tried to suppress or ignore something you've done that you knew to be wrong? Maybe you hurt someone, lied, cheated, or broke a commandment. Maybe you're involved in something right now that you know is wrong. Whatever the case, you can fool people for a while. You can only fool yourself for a short time. And you can't fool God at all. You can justify the wrong and attempt to silence the guilt that gnaws on your conscience. But it still remains. Like a hidden sliver lurking below the skin, one day you'll bump it just right and OUCH! You're faced with that guilt again.

All the money you can throw into the offering plate won't buy off a guilty conscience. All the good deeds you can do won't quiet the accusations of a restless, condemning heart. You can help little old ladies cross the street, serve on the youth board, and go to church every Sunday until you are 110, and none of it will make any difference. Until you make a true and honest confession before God and receive his forgiveness, you will never escape the sin that hounds you. Confession needs to occur, followed by forgiveness, before you can walk away with a clean slate and be at peace. Then, having received God's gracious forgiveness, you will surely want to demonstrate the genuineness of your repentance by making restitution when necessary and appropriate. (Remember Zacchaeus? See Luke 19:8.)

The psalmist made it clear: A clean heart must come first before the joy of salvation is known. And that clean heart must be created by God:

Create in me a clean heart, O God,
  and put a new and right spirit within me.
Cast me not away from thy presence,
  and take not thy holy Spirit from me.
Restore to me the joy of thy salvation,
  and uphold me with a willing spirit.

                                        Psalm 51:10–12

Life with Others

There's a unique Lutheran community in the Transylvanian Alps of Romania that practices a beautiful custom connected to Communion. Each Saturday evening prior to a Communion service, the entire community shows up for a great reconciliation event. If anyone has done wrong to any other member during the preceding week, that person is expected to come clean on the spot in front of the whole community. If Natasha has stolen Babushka's laundry off the line, she is expected to confess right then and there before God and everybody. Not only that, she's expected to return it or make arrangements to buy Natasha some new undies. If Boris ran over Nicholai's pet pig, he's not only expected to confess it, he's expected to share the barbecue.

These Christians take seriously Christ's admonition to first be reconciled to each other before approaching the altar of God (Matthew 5:23–24). How can we expect to know oneness with God if we are still living in brokenness with each other? Only when our relationships with others are restored are we ready to commune. Only with oneness between people properly in place, can we go to the table with a clear conscience.

How does Communion bring life? It heals brokenness between people and enables them to make amends. That's life.

Life with Ourselves

Sin cannot be eradicated by a self-help course. You can read the Bible until you are blind, study the writings of every religious guru who ever lived, and lock yourself away in a monastery to try to escape sin. But still it will find you. It's too pervasive. It's too much a part of us. Sin is a cancer that survives every surgery, a virus that will outlast every treatment. It cannot be dealt with through any outside mechanism. It is a stain that grows not from the outside but from within. It can only be washed away from within. It can only be cleansed by the power of the living, restoring God. And that's exactly what occurs in our hearts when our Savior is present—touchable and forgiving—in, with, and under the bread and the wine.

It starts with confessing our sin and admitting our weakness. It ends in wholeness and life.

Salvation
Salvage

Trash used to be taken to an open-air landfill commonly referred to as the dump. If someone dug through the dump, picked up a promising item, cleaned it, and put it back into circulation, the item was considered salvaged. How can a broken, discarded piece of garbage gain value? If someone picks it up and values it, it has value. And if it is valued, it is valuable.

How can a broken and discarded life gain value? If God picks it up, cleans it, and puts it to good use, it has been given immense value. If God values it, it is valuable. That's what God is all about. God is in the salvage business! And the value of you is not what anyone else thinks you are worth. The value of you is what you are worth to God.

You are worth the life of his Son.

Pie in the Sky?

Some people think that the word *salvation* refers simply to a "pie in the sky in the sweet by-and-by"—

that salvation happens out there in heaven somewhere. But salvation is much more relevant than that! Eternity begins today. You don't have to wait until you have your funeral behind you to begin your eternity with God. Think of it! If God is alive in the "here and now" and you are alive in the "here and now," then your eternity with God begins today, in the "here and now." You can close your eyes each night in the presence of God and awake each new day to the presence of God. Every breath, every heartbeat, every sunrise is another beginning in your eternity with God.

St. Paul made it clear that salvation is here and now. He wrote: "For the word of the cross is folly to those who are perishing, but to us who are being saved it is the power of God" (1 Corinthians 1:18).

"To us who are being saved . . ." Paul makes it sound like salvation is an ongoing process. Guess what? It is. Salvation means wholeness, completeness. It begins in the here and now and is perfected in heaven.

Salvation and Community

When a whole community of faith comes together to clean out the garbage and confess their sin before God and each other, amazing things happen. Enemies become friends. Grudges melt away. Brokenness is healed. Relationships bound for the garbage heap can be salvaged. If God has forgiven them, they can rise and forgive each other. Communion with Christ brings salvation not only to our immortal souls. It can bring salvation to our relationships. Our families. Our communities.

There is nothing magical or mystical about this aspect of Communion. When people open themselves to each other and God, desiring at the depth of who they are to be healed and restored, grace is at work. The meal becomes the medium, the catalyst, the vehicle through which Christ brings us together to be refreshed and restored. It is as simple and complex as that.

Salvaging relationships in the here and now—that's part of the salvation life Communion brings.

Thought Time

1. Look at the following Scripture passages. Which one stands out most clearly to you when you think of confession and forgiveness? Why?

• "My power is made perfect in weakness" (2 Corinthians 12:9).

• "If we confess our sins, he is faithful and just, and will forgive our sins and cleanse us from all unrighteousness" (1 John 1:9).

• "Behold, I stand at the door and knock; if any one hears my voice and opens the door, I will come in to him and eat with him, and he with me" (Revelation 3:20).

• "I came that they may have life, and have it abundantly" (John 10:10).

• "Ask, and it will be given you; seek, and you will find; knock, and [the door] will be opened to you" (Matthew 7:7).

• "As far as the east is from the west, so far does he remove our transgressions from us" (Psalm 103:12).

2. How are the words *salve* and *salvage* related to the word *salvation?*

3. In one sentence state how you see forgiveness of sins bringing life and salvation.

CHAPTER 5

Some Questions

Who should receive Communion?

Sinners.

Penitent sinners.

Penitent sinners who desire forgiveness.

Penitent sinners who desire forgiveness and believe Christ's words "given and shed for you for the forgiveness of sins."

Pretty simple, huh?

Why should I take Communion?

In one sense, a Christian takes Holy Communion because Jesus said, "This do."

Jesus didn't say: "You might sometime possibly consider taking this and even eating it every once in a while to sort of remember me if you have the time."

He was a tad more directive than that. He said: "Take, eat. . . . This do in remembrance of me." Pretty clear words. And he was clear about this because he knows us. He knows what we need, even when we don't. His words are not a burdensome "do this or else!" Rather, when he says, "This do in remembrance of me" it's just another way of saying, "Come to me, all who labor and are heavy laden, and I will give you rest" (Matthew 11:28). Should you come to him—in prayer, in worship, in Holy Communion? Yes. You're invited. Jesus says, "Come."

Do I have to feel right to go?

Sometimes people think that they have done something too terrible for even God to forgive. They refrain from coming to the altar because they feel unworthy. Luther taught that it was precisely when a person felt unworthy and sorry for sin that he or she was best prepared to go to Communion.

If, on the other hand, you are having a quarrel with someone and feel hatred, anger, resentment, or jealousy, you do well first to go and make peace with that person. (Remember those Transylvanian Lutherans?) The apostle Paul believed strongly in getting rid of resentments before receiving the Sacrament. It is not only hypocritical to carry resentment and bitterness up to the altar with you, it is downright dangerous!

First confess your sins to each other and forgive each other. Then you can go up to the altar with a clear conscience.

Why do some churches celebrate Communion weekly, while others celebrate it weakly?

To some folks, taking Communion once a month seems about right. Why? Because that's what they grew up with.

People who grew up Roman Catholic are used to celebrating Mass every week. Going to church means going to Mass. Forgiveness and restoration between God and others is a natural part of their weekly ritual. Many don't feel like they've been to a real church service unless they've had Communion.

In other traditions Communion is held only a handful of times each year. To those folks, taking Communion more frequently would rob it of its uniqueness.

In pioneer days there was a good reason for having Communion infrequently. Many immigrant settlements were served by a single itinerant, circuit-riding preacher. If you could only have Communion when the preacher was in town, and the preacher only rode up on his horse but once a month, that's how often you'd get Communion.

The Lord doesn't give us hard-and-fast rules about how often to take Communion, the type of wine or bread to use, or whether to be in a cathedral or in the woods. What matters most to God is the condition of the heart.

If your heart is humble, if you are sorry for your sins and deeply desire Christ's forgiving presence to cleanse and restore you, then you can take Communion as often as you like. You are certainly welcome. Christ won't turn you away.

How often should I take Holy Communion?

How often do you need the reinforcing touch of Christ's love and an audible assurance of forgiveness? How often do you wish to be cleansed and fresh before God? That's how often you can take Communion.

The writer of Hebrews wrote: "Therefore, since we are surrounded by so great a cloud of witnesses, let us also lay aside every weight, and sin which clings so closely, and let us run with perseverance the race that is set before us, looking to Jesus . . ." (12:1–2).

It is as if the angels along with all the saints in heaven are sitting together in the grandstands cheering us on. We are surrounded by them, and as each sin is cast aside, a roar goes up from the stands. How often do you wish to run the race? That's how often you can take Communion.

Weeks sometimes speed by with few challenges or problems. Then, all of a sudden, you find yourself up to your neck in need. Illness, challenges with friends, discouragement, and defeat come your way, and you grope for a power greater than your own to lead you through it all. How often do you need to kneel in the presence of God and receive Christ's restoring presence? That's how often you can take Communion.

Are there instances when someone should not commune?

Sad to say, yes, there are: two situations, to be precise. First, if you refuse to admit to God that you are a sinner or if you refuse to forgive another sinner who has wronged you, then the pastor, acting for the congregation, would have to tell you not to come to the table. Why? Because choosing to be unforgiving or unrepentant is choosing not to be a part of the Christian community. Communion is intended only for repentant, forgiving members of the Lord's family.

There is a second reason someone should not commune. It has to do with the divisions that have broken Jesus' church into denominations. One denomination teaches what another rejects. One congregation can't tolerate what another believes. Christian believers, tragically, are divided over what they will teach in their pulpits and Sunday school classrooms. By selecting to be part of a congregation and denomination that teaches God's message from the Bible and presents his sacraments in a particular way, you are placing yourself in a fellowship that does not agree with interpretations that other denominations and congregations hold. (You are not saying that they are not Christians!)

Wherever such divisions exist, they need to be healed, not ignored. Coming to Communion with people from other denominations that teach and believe differently than we do or going to Communion at their altars isn't going to take away the divisions. This has led to the practice of close Communion, that is, ordinarily inviting only those people to the Sacrament who are united in the confession of faith. We are looking forward to that great day when Jesus comes back to invite us to heaven. Then he will unite all people who believe in him. We will sit down together at the banquet table of eternal life.

What attitude should I take up with me to Communion?

There is a serious side to Communion, which we should never forget. The gift of forgiveness comes at the great cost of Jesus' life and blood. To free us from sin, the Son of God faced torture on the cross. His body was broken in our place. His blood was shed to pay the price for our sin. This is a serious matter and must not be taken lightly. This aspect of Communion does demand careful and prayerful thought.

But precisely because of these sad and serious facts, we can shout, sing, and celebrate! It is precisely because of Christ's sorrowful death that our lives can be filled

41

with joy! We were lost. Now in Christ we are found. We were once condemned. Now we are free. We were doomed to return to the dust. In his resurrection we will live forever. We once faced life alone. In Christ we can now experience the very presence of God.

Whenever we share the meal, our risen Lord comes again and again—in, with, and under the bread and wine—to fill us with confidence, forgiveness, and hope. Christ himself is ours. What attitude does all this call for? I like to call it a great and serious joy!

A Final Thought

How can Spirit be known to flesh? It cannot. Yet, that is precisely the point of Christ. God chose to come in flesh and blood—as Savior, not judge—so that we could come into God's presence as dear children come to their dear father. And to those who ache for God's embrace, that's what can happen in this holy sacrament. In the bread and the wine, God's love and forgiveness are placed on our lips. And in that moment of faith and mystery, our awareness is heightened, our senses are aroused, our sins are forgiven, and our spirits come into the presence of the living God.

> In hope I come to your high table,
> Your testament of deepest love;
> For by its grace I now am able
> To know the heart of God above.
> *Lutheran Worship* 242:4

Joy is the surprise that meets us at the table of Holy Communion. A great and serious joy. When we kneel and come clean before God something miraculous happens. God's promise of forgiveness ekes into our secret need for restoration, and WHAM! Grace and joy! In the bread and the wine we don't simply encounter some theoretical concept of forgiveness. We taste it with our tongue and with our heart. We touch it with our hand and with our spirit. We feel it with our fingers and with our faith. And the hunger and thirst for righteousness—for that clean and right relationship with God—is filled.

The prodigal son thought he'd have to be a servant for the rest of his life as he walked back up that long and winding road to his father's house. Then before he knew what hit him, surprise! He was back in the family and Dad was throwing a party.

The lost sheep probably figured he'd get a kick in the behind for wandering away and causing the boss to lose a night's sleep. Then, before he knew what hit him, surprise! He was being gently carried to the fold in the arms of the good shepherd.

We may think we deserve a ticket to hell for the things we've done (and—honesty confesses—yes, we do). Yet suddenly Jesus stands before us at his table with a loaf in one hand and a cup in the other, and surprise! "Come and eat, friend. You're welcome at my side. Get washed up. It's time for dinner."

Relief. Freedom. Joy. Life.

Wow!

Final Thought Time
A Personal Preparation

To be properly prepared to receive the Lord's Supper, a short period of self-examination before each service is often quite helpful. This may be done at home during a quiet time the night before, in the sanctuary just prior to the service, or during an organized prayer time in the service itself. The following are some short questions you may wish to ask yourself prior to receiving Communion so that you will be properly prepared.

• Do I believe that Jesus has paid the price to forgive my sins and the sins of the whole world? Do I believe that Jesus will forgive my sins? (Read 1 John 1:9–2:2.)

• Do I honestly trust the words that say Christ's body and blood are given for me and shed for me—for the forgiveness of my sins?

• What are some areas in my life where I need God's forgiveness?

• What are some areas in my life where I need the forgiveness of others?

• Am I sorry for my sins and willing to confess them to God?

• Am I willing to ask forgiveness from and make restitution to those I have wronged?

• Am I willing to give forgiveness now to all those who have wronged me and let go of my bitterness?

• Am I presently angry, jealous, or upset with anyone?

• Am I willing to accept the forgiveness Christ offers and rise to live as a new, forgiven, forgiving person?

If you truly believe Christ's body and blood were sacrificed for the forgiveness of *your* sins and that Jesus comes to you in the bread and wine offering complete forgiveness, then your sins *are* forgiven.

Go through this personal examination in your mind each time you are about to receive the Sacrament. If it is helpful, write a sentence answering each question. Be as honest and specific as you can. When you're through, ask God to forgive those sins you've confessed, to restore the broken relationships you are involved in, and to help you find the great and serious joy of a clear conscience.